ISLAMIC C

BY ATIF TOOR

Rourke

Publishing LLC
Vero Beach, Florida 32964

Developed by Nancy Hall, Inc., for Rourke Publishing.
© 2006 Nancy Hall, Inc.

Acknowledgments are listed on page 48.

www.rourkepublishing.com

Photo research by L. C. Casterline
Design by Atif Toor and Iram Khandwala

Library of Congress Cataloging-In-Publication Data

Toor, Atif, 1971-
  Islamic culture / by Atif Toor.
     p. cm. -- (Discovering the arts)
  Includes bibliographical references and index.
  ISBN 1-59515-521-X (hardcover)
  1. Arts, Islamic--Juvenile literature. I. Title. II. Series.
  NX688.A5T66 2006
  709'.17'67--dc22
                          2005010950

Title page: The Dome of the Rock, Jerusalem, Ummayad Dynasty.
The calligraphy on the walls of the Dome of the Rock proclaimed Islam's
place among the major faiths of the world, along with Christianity and Judaism.

Printed in the USA
10 9 8 7 6 5 4 3 2 1

CONTENTS

INTRODUCTION: **The Rise of Islam**   4

CHAPTER 1: **Early Islam**   6

CHAPTER 2: **Islam in Africa**   14

CHAPTER 3: **Out of Asia**   20

CHAPTER 4: **The Ottomans and Safavids**   30

CHAPTER 5: **The Mughals of India**   34

CHAPTER 6: **Islamic Culture Today**   38

TIMELINE   44

GLOSSARY   45

FURTHER READING   46

INDEX   47

ACKNOWLEDGMENTS   48

THE RISE OF ISLAM

In C.E. 610, a man was praying in a small cave on a mountain near Mecca. When he returned to the city, he described a vision he'd had. The angel Jibra'il (Gabriel) had come to him, with a message from God. The man's name was Muhammad. The vision he shared with the people of Arabia (now Saudi Arabia) gave birth to a new faith called Islam.

In Muhammad's time, most Arabs worshipped many gods. The leaders of Mecca feared that their gods would be angered by Muhammad's teachings about the One God (*Allah* in Arabic). Because of this, he left Mecca in 622 and went to Yathrib, which later became the city of

Many Islamic cultures do not allow images of Muhammad, but some do. For example, the Ottoman rulers of Turkey hired artists to create paintings for books about Muhammad's life. This painting from the 1500s shows Muhammad and the angel Jibra'il.

Calligraphy, a type of writing, is the most respected art form in Islam. It is used to decorate pottery, metalwork, buildings, and textiles as well as to write books.

Medina. In 630, Muhammad and an army of followers returned and conquered Mecca.

For the next 100 years, Arab armies led by **caliphs** carried the message of Islam to new lands. They spread out eastward from Arabia to Iran, Central Asia, northern India, northwest China, and Southeast Asia, and west to North Africa and Spain. Throughout Islamic lands, the language of the faith remained Arabic, and all Muslims practiced the Islamic way of life in the same basic way. The Islamic people, however, often adopted the customs of the local culture. These blended cultures gave birth to new forms of art, music, science, and literature.

In the 1800s, much of the Islamic world was taken over by European powers. As a faith, however, Islam continues to grow. Today, it is practiced by more than a billion people throughout the world. The story of Islamic art and culture is not the story of just one country and its people, but of many.

CHAPTER 1

EARLY ISLAM

Every year, millions of people travel to Mecca. One of the first things they do is circle the Ka'aba seven times and then pray.

It is said that the **prophet** Abraham built the first Ka'aba in Mecca as a house of the One God. Inside the cube-shaped building is a meteorite called the Black Stone, which dates back to Adam, the first man. After Abraham, images of many gods were placed there. When Muhammad returned to Mecca, he cleared them all away and declared the place holy to Allah. From then on, Muslims would face toward the *qibla*, or in the direction of the Ka'aba, when they prayed.

All Muslim people follow the Five Pillars of Islam. First they must declare their faith by saying "There is no god but God; Muhammad is the messenger of God," in Arabic. Second, they must face Mecca at five set times a day to pray. Third, they must give to the poor. Fourth, they must not eat or drink between dawn and sunset during the Muslim month of Ramadan. Fifth, they must travel to Mecca at least once during their lifetime. This trip is called *hajj*.

Arabic calligraphy is written from right to left and can take many different forms. This Qur'an was written using *nashki*, a type of calligraphy that may have been invented by Ibn al-Bawwab around the late 900s.

Muslims regard the **Qur'an**, Allah's words as spoken by Jibra'il, as the final book of sacred writings that began with the Jews and Christians. During Muhammad's lifetime, the verses of the Qur'an were passed on by word of mouth. After his death in 632, the 114 chapters were written down in book form. Muhammad's sayings and thoughts on the meaning of the Qur'an are known as the *hadith*.

Because the Qur'an contains the direct words of God, great care is taken to copy the words exactly. However, copying the Qur'an inspired artists to create many forms of Arabic writing, called calligraphy. Though the Qur'an could be decorated with patterns and flower designs, it was never illustrated with pictures of humans or animals. This is partly due to the belief that only Allah can create beings that move, and artists should not try to take on God's role by drawing or painting figures. This rule, however, does not always hold true for non-religious works.

The Dome of the Rock, Jerusalem. The original dome was copper. Today, it is covered with 24-karat gold.

In 661, Muawiya claimed his place as caliph and founded the Umayyad **dynasty**, or ruling family. The capital was moved from Mecca to Damascus (in present-day Syria). In Muslim lands, Jews, Christians, and others were allowed to practice their faiths, but they had to pay a tax called the *jizya*. With the money from the *jizya* and other taxes, the fifth Umayyad caliph, Abd al-Malik, began to put up buildings in the major cities.

One of the earliest Muslim buildings still standing is the Dome of the Rock in Jerusalem. Completed in 691, the **shrine** is a memorial to Muhammad's night journey with Jibra'il from Mecca, to Jerusalem, to heaven, and back again. The eight-sided building is topped by a dome, supported by marble columns, and decorated with tiles.

Muhammad's home in Medina had also served as a prayer hall. The house had an open space where Muslims could sit in rows and pray toward the Ka'aba. During the early 700s, an alcove called a **mihrab** was added to the wall facing Mecca. At each of the four corners, a **minaret** was built. From

Mosaic landscapes decorate the walls inside the Great Mosque of Damascus.

these tall towers, a **muezzin** would give the call to prayer. The layout of many **mosques**, Muslim houses of worship, follows the same basic plan.

The Umayyad caliph al-Walid built the Great Mosque in Damascus on the site of a former Christian church. Finished in 715, the mosque is decorated with thousands of glass tiles. These form a **mosaic** of detailed patterns and landscapes, as well as quotes from the Qur'an. As in the Qur'an, animals and people are never pictured in mosques.

After Muhammad died, Abu Bakr was elected caliph. Some people, however, thought that Muhammad's son-in-law Ali should be caliph. They became known as Shi'i Muslims. People who thought caliphs should be elected were called Sunni Muslims. The split between them grew deeper in 680 when Muhammad's grandson Hussein and his family were killed by the Umayyads in the battle of Karbala. Shi'is mark Hussein's death each year with parades, poetry, and sad songs during the Islamic month of Muharram. His faithful white horse, Zuljana, is also honored. Today, about ten percent of all Muslims, including most Iranians and Iraqis, are Shi'i.

ISLAMIC SPAIN

Like other mosques, the Great Mosque of Córdoba has a *mihrab* set into the wall that faces Mecca.

Under the Umayyad dynasty, Muslims from North Africa crossed the Strait of Gibraltar and invaded Spain in 711. When the Abbasids came to power, the last Umayyad prince, Abd al-Rahman I, fled to Spain. He declared himself ruler and made Córdoba his capital city. It would become one of the greatest centers of learning in Europe. As in other Muslim countries, Christians and Jews were allowed to practice their faith in peace.

Al-Rahman I began building the Great Mosque of Córdoba in 785. A courtyard planted with regular rows of orange trees gave way to a dim inside "forest" of columns. Through the columns could be seen the *mihrab* with its golden mosaic tiles. Today, the mosque is a Christian cathedral.

Córdoba fell to the Christians in 1238. Not long afterward, rulers of the Muslim Nasrid dynasty began building the Alhambra, a fortress city in Granada. Building would continue for 250 years. Rising from a hilltop, the forbidding stone walls of the fortress hide the beautiful palaces and gardens within. Channels of water flow through the palaces, cooling the air, and pass into courtyards with fountains. Tall, lacy-looking arches supported by narrow columns provide a covered area linking the outside with the inside. The play of light and shadow changes throughout the day.

In 1492, after 700 years of Muslim rule, Christian forces under King Ferdinand and Queen Isabella drove the Muslims out of Spain.

The Court of the Lions in the Alhambra palace

The Muslims of Islamic Spain, which is also known as al-Andalus, introduced advances in science, music, and agriculture to Europe. They brought irrigation systems from Syria and Arabia that changed the dry landscape of southern Spain. They also introduced many new foods, including rice, sugarcane, eggplant, pomegranates, peaches, lemons, and oranges. The word *orange* comes from the Arabic word *naranj*.

This painting from a book written by al-Mutadibih in 1214 shows the anatomy of the eye.

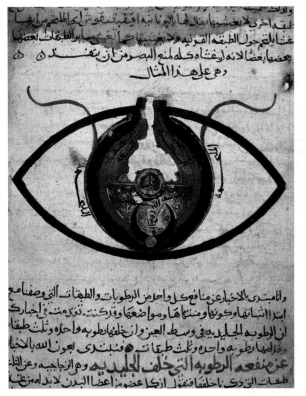

The Abbasid dynasty came to power after 749 and moved the capital east to Baghdad (in modern Iraq) on the Tigris River. At this time, the Islamic world stretched from Spain, across much of northern Africa to the Middle East, and into parts of Asia and India. Unlike other Islamic cities that were densely packed with buildings, Baghdad was carefully planned. The city's palace and mosque stood in the center of a great open circle. Around them were rings of government offices, houses, and shops. The entire city was protected by tall mud-brick walls.

For the next 500 years, Baghdad was the center of Islamic education and culture. In the 800s, traders brought paper west from China. Soon it was being widely used in all kinds of books. Works on science, astronomy, and poetry were illustrated, some with simple drawings and others with richly detailed miniature paintings.

In Baghdad during the 800s, al-Khawarizmi, the mathematician, wrote *Kitab al-Jabr*, the book that laid the foundation for modern algebra. Here, too, **scholars** and students translated the works of ancient Greek thinkers such as Aristotle and Plato. In Europe, these works were forgotten during the Middle Ages (about 400 to 1400). Without the Islamic translations, they would have been lost.

In Samarra, another great city north of Baghdad, carved stucco (a type of plaster) decoration hid the mud-brick walls. Later, molds were pressed against the wet stucco to make repeating designs. Among the designs were **geometric** shapes, such as circles, squares, and stars, and the fanciful plant shapes that were later called **arabesques** in the west.

In 1258, the armies of Hülegü, the grandson of the great Mongol warrior Genghis Khan, overran Baghdad, killing thousands of its citizens. The Mongols looted and destroyed the city's libraries, museums, and treasures. This marked the end of a central power in the Islamic world.

The mosque built in Samarra by Caliph al-Mutawakkil in 852 was once the largest mosque in the world. Its spiral minaret is about 170 feet (50 m) tall.

The One Thousand and One Nights (also known as *The Arabian Nights*) was first written down in Arabic in the mid 800s. The stories are set in places like India, China, Iran, and Arabia. They are told by a princess named Sheherezad to entertain her husband, King Shehryar. Among the most popular tales are "Sinbad the Sailor," "Ali Baba and the Forty Thieves," and "Aladdin." At left, Sinbad and the old man of the sea are shown in a painting from a book created in 1399.

CHAPTER 2

ISLAM IN AFRICA

The mosque of al-Azhar, built in al-Qahira in 970, was a center of learning for Shi'i students. Today, al-Azhar University is considered one of the world's oldest universities.

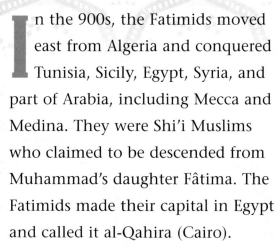

In the 900s, the Fatimids moved east from Algeria and conquered Tunisia, Sicily, Egypt, Syria, and part of Arabia, including Mecca and Medina. They were Shi'i Muslims who claimed to be descended from Muhammad's daughter Fâtima. The Fatimids made their capital in Egypt and called it al-Qahira (Cairo).

The city was well placed for trade between India and the countries bordering the Mediterranean Sea and became rich. The palaces of the Fatimid rulers contained many treasures. For example, a map of the world made in 964 was woven in silk and decorated with gold and silver. In the courtyards, clockwork metal birds sang in metal trees.

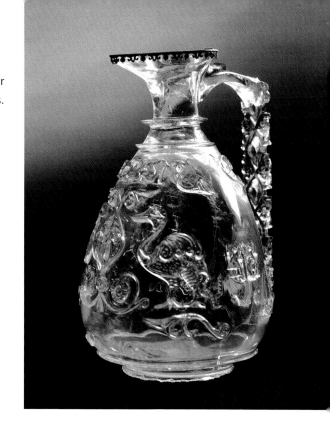

This beautifully carved rock crystal pitcher from Egypt dates back to the late 900s.

Lustreware was first made in Iraq, but became the most popular type of pottery in Egypt and Syria. Lustreware pottery was glazed and fired in a kiln (oven). It was then painted with metallic paint and fired again to bond the paint to the glaze. The metallic paint made the pottery shine. Many lustreware pieces were signed by the potter, and some noted where they were made.

Fatimid **artisans** were also skilled in many other areas. They made containers from hollowed-out and carved **rock crystal**, fashioned fine jewelry from gold, and created detailed wood carvings.

Beginning in 1095 and lasting for about 200 years, Christian armies from Europe tried to take Jerusalem and other holy lands back from the Muslims. These wars, called the Crusades, began an exchange of goods and ideas between the Muslim world and Europe. In this torn painting from the 1100s, Fatimid troops are setting out from a fortress to attack Crusaders.

This brass canteen inlaid with silver was made in the 1200s. It shows scenes from the Bible, and experts think it was sold as a souvenir to Christian crusaders.

In 1171, the Fatimid rule came to an end when Salah al-Din (Saladin) defeated Crusaders attacking al-Qahira. Afterward, he took over Egypt and founded the Ayyubid dynasty. He replaced Shi'i practices with Sunni practices and opened the gates of the royal city of al-Qahira to the common people. By the 1180s, Salah al-Din had also gained control of Yemen and Syria. In 1182, he left Egypt to fight the Crusaders. In 1187, he took back Jerusalem after 88 years of Christian rule. Salah al-Din never returned to Egypt and died in Damascus.

Under the Ayyubid rulers, potters began making underglaze-painted wares. This pottery was painted first, then covered with a clear glaze. Instead of having to be fired twice in a kiln, like lustreware, it only had to be fired once. Ayyubid artisans were also known for their inlaid metalwork, enameled glass, and wood carvings.

During this time, women, too, became builders. For example, Rabia Khatun, Salah al-Din's sister, built a Sunni religious school, or **madrassa**, in Damascus. In al-Qahira, the Abbuyids built the Tomb of the Abbasid Caliphs for the caliphs who had fled Baghdad after the Mongols attacked it in 1258.

Mamluks, or slave soldiers, from Turkey worked for the Abbasids and other Islamic rulers, including the Ayyubids. These soldiers were educated and well trained. Though they were considered slaves, they were often paid and could hold important government jobs. In 1250, the Mamluks overthrew the last Ayyubid ruler and founded their own dynasty.

This picture of Salah al-Din was made several years after his death.

While many mosques have domes, minarets, and arches, others are built in the style of the local culture. In the 1200s, Koy Konboro, the first Islamic ruler of Djenné, Mali, built the Great Mosque of Djenné. Its walls were made of sun-dried mud bricks smoothed with mud plaster. Konboro's mosque fell into ruin but was rebuilt in 1906. Today, it is the largest mud-brick building in the world. Every year, the townspeople gather to give the mosque a new coat of mud plaster.

The *Kalila wa Dimna* is a book of fables first written down during the 300s and still read today. In this Mamluk painting from 1354, Fairuz the hare is fooling the king of the elephants into thinking that the moon he sees in the water is speaking to him.

The Mamluks kept the Mongols out of Egypt. They also stopped them from taking over Syria and other Islamic lands at the eastern end of the Mediterranean Sea. The Mamluks would remain in power for almost 300 years. Under them, al-Qahira became the greatest Islamic city. Though the Abbasids were still caliphs, they worked under the Mamluks and were no longer rulers.

Mamluk rulers hired calligraphers to produce beautiful Qur'ans, some more than 3 feet (1 m) in height. Others might run to as many as 30 volumes. On each page, there might be only a few lines of text surrounded by decoration.

Under the Mamluks, skilled craftspeople continued to make glassware, pottery, inlaid metalwork, and wood carvings. They were best known, however, for their enameled and gilded glassware, which was first made in the days of the

This enameled glass lamp is from the Mosque of Sultan Hasan in al-Qahira.

Ayyubids. After a glass container was blown, gold or enamel (colored glass that has been powdered) was applied to the surface with a brush or pen. The glass was then fired in a kiln to fix the colors. This type of glass was later made in Venice, Italy.

The Mamluks were also well known for their textiles and large, brightly colored carpets. The carpets were hand-knotted out of wool and had one or more geometric **medallions** in the center. Around the medallions, every square inch was filled with shapes such as stars, triangles, and octagons. Arabesques filled in any empty spaces.

Ibn Battuta was born in Tangier, Morocco. In 1325, at age 21, he set out for Mecca and wound up traveling for about 30 years. He covered 75,000 miles (120,700 km), visiting India, China, Arabia, and West and East Africa. Toward the end of his life, the story of his travels was written down in a book called *Rihla* (*Travels*).

CHAPTER 3

OUT OF ASIA

In 1206, the inventor al-Jazari finished his book *Al-Jami Bain Al-Ilm Wal-Amal Al-Nafi Fi Sinat'at Al-Hiyal* (*The Book of Knowledge of Ingenious Mechanical Devices*). In it, he described 50 machines, such as this fountain.

In the late 900s, two dynasties founded by Turkish soldiers from Central Asia gained power. The Seljuks defeated the Ghaznavids in 1038 and then took over Baghdad in 1055. The Abbasid caliphs remained in place but were ruled by the Seljuks. Soon, the Seljuks had conquered all of Iran, Iraq, Syria, and Anatolia (present-day Turkey).

Under the Seljuks, artisans produced metalwork of very high quality. Bronze and brass objects were inlaid with gold, silver, copper, and black enamel called **niello**. Incense burners were often shaped like animals. Many were decorated with figures and calligraphy. At this time, pictures of animals or objects were sometimes made entirely out of calligraphy. These were called **calligrams**.

The Silk Road was really a number of trade routes that connected China to Europe through central Asia. Silks, spices, and other goods from

In caravansaries like the Sultan Han Caravansary in Cappadocia, Turkey, the Seljuks allowed traders to stay for three days at no charge. There they could see a doctor, get their shoes repaired, have their animals cared for, and more—also for free.

China traveled thousands of miles by camel caravan to be exchanged for wool, linen, and other goods from Africa and Europe. The Seljuks built large stone buildings called **caravansaries** along the routes. Here, merchants and their animals could safely stop and rest.

Several English words for fine fabrics come from Persian (the language spoken in Iran) and Arabic: The cotton fabric called muslin got its name from the city of Mosul in Iraq. The word *damask*, used for a patterned fabric, comes from Damascus. Mohair, a soft wool fabric, is taken from *mukhayyir*, the Arabic word for "choice, select." Taffeta comes from the Persian word *taftan*, which means "to spin."

Mina'i (enameled) pottery was invented in Iran about 1170. This kind of pottery was colorful and often pictured people and animals. First the pottery was painted with blue, then glazed and fired in a kiln. Then more colors were added and the piece was glazed and fired again. During Seljuk times, pictures of the zodiac signs and the planets were popular. In the bottom of the *Mina'i* bowl at left the sun is surrounded by symbols for the moon and the planets Venus, Jupiter, Mars, Mercury, and Saturn.

POETRY AND SCIENCE

In your light I learn how to love.
In your beauty, how to make poems.
You dance inside my chest,
where no one sees you,
but sometimes I do,
and that sight becomes this art.

—Rumi

Ibn Sena, who was born in 980, became a scholar in Iran. He wrote poetry as well as books on science and medicine. *Kitab al-Shifa* (*The Book of Healing*) was an encyclopedia of religion and science. *Al-Qanun al-Tibb* (*The Canon of Medicine*) was a five-volume book on medicine. Both were used in Europe for several hundred years.

Omar Khayyam was born in Nishapur, Iran, in 1048. Today, he is best known in the West for the *Rubaiyat*, a book of poems. However, Khayyam was also a mathematician who wrote a book on algebra and studied the stars.

Abu'l Qasim Mansur, who used the pen name Firdausi, wrote the *Shahnama* (*The Book of Kings*) in about 1000. Made up of about 30,000 verses, it told the history of Iran through stories of kings and heroes. Later,

These two pages are from a copy of *al-Qanun al-Tibb* by Ibn Sena that was made in the 1300s.

This painting was created in the late 1500s to illustrate *Bustan* (*Garden*) or *Gulistan* (*Rose Garden*), which were written in the late 1200s by the Sufi poet Shaykh Muslihuddin Sa'di. It shows Mevlevi dervishes dancing while a meal is being prepared.

the *Shahnama* would be illustrated with beautiful miniature paintings.

Some Muslims followed their own path to Islam through Sufism. Many Sufis used poetry set to music to spread the message of Islam. Often in their poems, romantic love stands for deep religious belief. Shortly after Jelaluddin Rumi was born in 1207, his family moved to Anatolia. There he practiced Sufism and wrote poetry. Rumi had many followers, and after he died, they formed the Sufi group called the Mevlevi dervishes. They are sometimes called "whirling dervishes," because they spin in circles as part of their spiritual practice.

The *ud* is a stringed instrument that was often played when someone recited poetry. Paintings of musicians playing the *ud* have been found on bowls from Iraq dating back to the 700s. The *ud* reached Europe during the Crusades and is the ancestor of the lute. Today, the *ud* is still popular in the Middle East and North Africa.

From Mongolia, fierce warriors on horseback led by Genghis Khan swept across Asia, conquering every land in their path. After Genghis Khan died, his sons and grandsons took over. By the mid-1200s, they ruled all the lands in Asia from China to the Middle East and in Europe as far west as Hungary.

After conquering Baghdad in 1258, Hülegü became the ruler of all the Islamic lands. His brother, Kublai Khan, who was called the Great Khan, ruled China. Hülegü took the name Il-Khan, meaning "lesser Khan," and founded the Ilkhanid dynasty. His summer capital was in Tabriz, Iran, and his winter capital was in Baghdad. In 1295, under the Ilkhanid ruler Ghazan, Islam became the state religion.

Genghis Khan is shown fighting the Chinese in this miniature painting from a 1397 version of the *Shahnama* by Firdausi.

The central part of this tile from the Takht-i Sulaiman palace pictures a phoenix, a bird taken from Chinese myth.

The Mongols were nomads who moved from place to place. They liked beautiful things that were small enough to carry or wear. After their conquests, the Mongols built palaces but still moved between them in large royal tents. These tents were not taken down but were mounted on wheels and pulled by oxen. Fine textiles lined the insides of the tents, and beautiful wool carpets covered the floors.

Under Mongol leadership, it became safe to travel the Silk Road, and trade grew between China and the Islamic lands. Artists and artisans, too, moved from one place to another. Styles and traditions from China began to appear in Islamic art. Dragons, phoenixes, and other figures from Chinese myth were pictured on Ilkhanid pottery and tiles, such as those on the inside walls of the Takht-i Sulaiman palace. The palace walls were also decorated with gold- and lustre-painted tiles that made the walls sparkle in the light.

This gold Mongol bracelet with a turquoise stone is decorated with calligraphy.

Under Ilkhanid rulers, the art of manuscript painting reached new heights. In the early 1300s, Rashid al-Din wrote a history of the Mongols, beginning with Genghis Khan. It was called *Jami' al-Tavarikh* (*Collected Histories*). The illustrations combine several styles, including Iranian, Chinese, and Christian.

In this picture from *Jami' al-Tavarikh* by Rashid al-Din, warriors of the Iranian army are dressed like Mongols and use Mongol weapons.

The Ilkhanids did not frown on religious images and even allowed pictures of Muhammad, though his face was often hidden behind a veil.

The Great Mongol *Shahnama* was probably created in the 1330s. It may be one of the first illustrated versions. As in the *Jami' al-Tavarikh*, the paintings, which completely cover the large pages, combine several different styles. In both books, all the people, Mongol or not, have Mongol features and hairstyles. Their clothes, weapons, and furniture look like those used by the Ilkhanids.

By the early 1400s, a Turkish-Mongol ruler called Timur (Tamerlane) had gained control of central Asia, Iran, Iraq, Syria, and parts of Anatolia and India. Timur brought artisans from conquered lands, especially Iran, to the Timurid capitals of Samarkand (in Uzbekistan) and Herat (in Afghanistan). The Timurids built large palaces, mosques, and Sufi shrines marked by their size, double domes, and minarets. Women as well as men were builders during this time. In Samarkand, Timur's wife Bibi Khanum built a *madrassa* next to the mosque that is often called by her name.

In Samarkand, a group of tombs called Shah-i Zinda was built for members of Timur's family. The name, which means "living king," refers to Kusam ibn Abbas, a cousin of Muhammad. According to legend, Abbas brought Islam to the area in the 600s and is buried there.

CARPETS & TEXTILES

Many Arabs, Seljuks, Mongols, and other Islamic peoples were nomads. Their homes were tents and their furniture and floor coverings were carpets and pillows. Carpet weaving began as a nomadic craft. Rugs were hand-knotted by families on small wood looms, which could be easily carried along.

By the 1500s, carpet weaving had moved to cities. Workshops housed large looms that could be used to weave huge carpets for the rich and for export to Europe. Textile and carpet making were the biggest industries in many Islamic lands up until the 1800s. India, Pakistan, Turkey, and Iran are still major exporters of hand-knotted carpets.

One of two silk-and-wool Ardabil carpets can be found in the Victoria & Albert Museum in London. Made in Iran during 1539 to 1540, it is 34.5 feet (10.5 m) long and 17.5 feet (5.3 m) wide and has more than 26 million hand-tied knots!

This red and gold robe belonged to the Ottoman ruler Bayezid II, who reigned from 1481 to 1512.

Like architecture and painting, Islamic textiles and carpets often feature detailed patterns taken from nature, geometry, and calligraphy. Carpet designs from Iran and India often include hunting scenes, gardens, and arabesques, rather like miniature paintings but on a larger scale. The amount of detail in a carpet depends on the number of knots used to make it. Large carpets often require millions of knots and can take months to complete.

Textiles still play an important role in Islamic culture. Most Muslims pray on mats made of woven fabric. Men may wear turbans or woven caps, and some women wear head coverings or veils as a sign of modesty. Loose-fitting cotton clothing is used for everyday wear, while heavily embroidered, expensive clothes are kept for special occasions such as weddings and holidays.

CHAPTER 4

THE OTTOMANS AND SAFAVIDS

Finished in 1617, the Mosque of Sultan Ahmet I in Constantinople was designed by the architect Sedefkâr Mehmet Agha, a student of Mimar Sinan. It is also called the Blue Mosque after the blue tiles that decorate the inside.

In Anatolia, the Ottoman dynasty was founded after the Seljuks lost power to the Mongols. In 1453, Mehmet II led the Ottomans in conquering the Christian city of Constantinople, now Istanbul. He had the great Hagia Sofia church turned into a mosque and built the Topkapi palace. Over the next 400 years, Ottoman rulers would continue adding to the palace, which became as large as a city.

By 1517, the Ottomans under Selim I had conquered all of Anatolia, as well as the Mamluks in Syria, Egypt, and western Arabia. Artists from Islamic lands and from all over Europe gathered at the royal Ottoman courts.

The art of the Ottomans reached its height in the mid-1500s during the reign of Suleyman, also known as Suleyman the Magnificent. He employed more than

This miniature portrait of Mehmet II was painted about 1480 by either Sinan Bey or his student Shiblizade Ahmed. One of Bey's teachers was Italian, and the use of Western shading can be seen in Mehmet's face and the folds of his clothes.

120 court artists. Architect Mimar Sinan designed hundreds of buildings during his career. He also built the Suleymaniye Mosque in Istanbul. This complex included a *madrassa*, an inn, a medical school, a hospital, a public bath, and a soup kitchen.

The wealth gained from Muslim conquests provided a huge supply of gold, silver, and precious stones. These were fashioned into jewelry and other objects. Suleyman once ordered a gold helmet that was adorned with 50 diamonds, 47 rubies, 27 emeralds, and 49 pearls.

During the 1500s, Iznik in Anatolia became famous for its pottery. Factories were controlled by the government. Though the pottery was produced in Iznik, royal artists in Istanbul created the designs, which the potters then transferred to the pieces. Many of the pieces pictured roses, tulips, and other flowers.

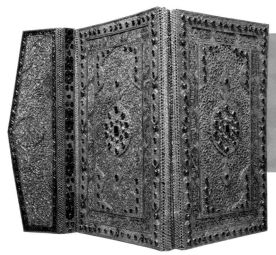

Ottoman rulers collected beautifully decorated objects and jewelry, which were guarded in royal treasuries. They stored a wealth of objects from around the world in the Topkapi palace. Today, the palace is a museum where visitors can see the royal collection. At left is a richly decorated Qur'an cover.

Kamal-uddin Bihzad was a master of miniature painting. This picture of a public bath, an illustration for *Khamsa*, written by the poet Nazimi, is full of movement and detail.

In 1501, Isma'il Safavi became the first ruler of the Safavid dynasty. By 1511, he controlled all of Iran. Under Safavid rule, the state religion changed from Sunni to Shi'i.

While the names of most miniature painters remained unknown, a few artists were celebrated for the high quality of their work. Kamal-uddin Bihzad's art was prized for its detail and rich colors. Bihzad first worked in the royal Timurid library in Herat. In 1510, he moved to the Iranian city of Tabriz and the court of Isma'il. Later, Bihzad became the royal librarian of Tabriz and trained other artists who influenced painting in Iran, Turkey, and India.

In 1587, Isma'il's great grandson, Shah Abbas, became the Safavid ruler. During his reign, single paintings became more popular than illustrated books because more people could afford them. Artists developed their own styles and began signing their work. Mu'in was born in 1617 and trained under the court master Reza Abbasi. Mu'in began by painting scenes from epic poems but went on to paint single-page pictures of everyday people.

This oil-on-canvas painting of Fath Ali Shah is by the head court painter Mirza Baba. The pocket watch on the carpet shows the time as eight o'clock. It was meant to let the viewer know that the painting captures the moment Ali Shah was crowned.

In the 1700s and 1800s, artists working under the Afsharid, Zand, and Qajar dynasties in Iran began using oil paints and working on life-sized portraits. This was a major change from the miniature paintings, which were done in watercolor. Artists were sent to Europe to study painting. The Qajar monarch Fath Ali Shah had large portraits of himself made, which combined European realism with the Islamic style of detailed patterns.

Beginning around 1600, most books were made in royal workshops. The artisans did everything from making the paper to binding the finished book. Calligraphers made their own pens and ink, then copied the text onto the pages, leaving room for art. Artists mixed their paints, and most had their own special skills. Some might paint only faces, while others might paint only battle scenes. Still other artists would paint frames around the pictures and add chapter titles and other decorations. When the pages were complete, they were sewn and bound.

THE MUGHALS OF INDIA

This miniature painting from about 1565 shows the court of Akbar. Musicians and Turkish dancers can be seen in the lower part of the picture.

Muslims ruled parts of India from the 600s until the 1800s. In the early 1500s, Zahiruddin Muhammad Babur and his army conquered India. A descendant of Timur, Babur founded the Mughal dynasty, which governed the country for nearly 400 years. The Mughals created a new style of art and architecture by blending Iranian and Indian traditions.

Like Iranian rulers, Mughal emperors supported a group of artists called a *karkhana*. Each group was led by a master artist called an *ustad*. The *ustad* trained apprentices to paint in the style wanted by the court. Early Mughal painting had highly detailed patterns, like the paintings of Iran. Scenes from poems and historical events were favored subject matter.

Later, Mughal emperors kept court artists. In the late 1500s, Akbar had more than 100. These artists attended

Mansur's paintings of birds and other animals were realistic as well as beautiful.

important ceremonies, were present at building sites, and even went to war. Court artists developed a more realistic style. Scenes of the court often included portraits of the emperors along with their guests and nobles. Each portrait was a true likeness of its subject.

Ustad Mansur began painting in the court of Akbar. Mansur was honored for his realistic paintings of plants and animals. He was also a favorite painter of Akbar's son, Emperor Jehangir, and was given the title Nadir-ul'Asr, or "Wonder of the Age."

As trade with Europe increased in the 1600s, European prints became available in India. Mughal painters began to use shading and perspective in their works. In Europe, Rembrandt and other artists began collecting and copying Mughal miniature paintings.

Some Islamic scholars frowned on singing and dancing as distracting Muslims from their faith. However, many Muslim cultures used singing and dancing in their religious practices. In India, Qawaali began in the 1300s as a Sufi form of music. It was used to spread the teachings of Islam throughout the country. A chorus of singers was accompanied by drums and a type of organ called a harmonium. Qawaali music is still popular. Nusrat Fateh Ali Khan (left) came from a family of Qawaali singers going back 600 years. He introduced new ideas to Qawaali music, and his recordings are enjoyed all over the world.

After the death of Jehangir, his son Shah Jahan became emperor. Like Akbar and Jehangir, he was a great supporter of the arts. He collected jewels and had a dagger made with a solid gold hilt and a sheath covered in 2,400 diamonds, rubies, and emeralds. His favorite branch of the arts, however, was architecture. Among his many building projects were a new city called Shajahanabad, the rebuilding of Akbar's red fort in Agra, and several mosques.

After the death of his favorite wife, Mumtaz Mahal, in 1631, he built her a white marble tomb on the banks of the Yamuna River in Agra. Completed in 1647, the beautiful Taj Mahal would become one of the most famous buildings in the world. It took thousands of artisans from Iran and India to build it.

On the side of the Taj Mahal opposite the river is a large garden built in the classic Islamic style. Two water channels cross in the center, dividing the garden

More than 2,500 pounds (1,134 kg) of gold and 500 pounds (227 kg) of precious stones were used to make the Peacock Throne for Shah Jahan. Today, the cost of making the throne would be well over 800 million dollars.

into four squares. Pathways divide each square into four more squares, making 16 flower beds. Paradise is described as a garden in the Qur'an. The well-designed architecture and gardens of the Taj Mahal reflect Shah Jahan's wish to create a paradise on Earth.

Building the Taj Mahal only cost half as much as making the Peacock Throne.

Muslim merchants from India brought Islam to the island country of Indonesia toward the end of the 1200s. There it existed with native beliefs, Hinduism, and other religions. At first, Muslim leaders did not want people to use the traditional puppets of the islands because they felt the images went against Islam. Because of that, people began to use *wayang kulit*, or shadow puppets. Since only the shadows of the puppets could be seen, the Muslim leaders approved them. Today, more Muslims live in Indonesia than anywhere else in the world.

ISLAMIC CULTURE
TODAY

An artist paints Islamic patterns on a ceramic vase before it is fired.

The 1800s and 1900s were a time of great change in the Islamic world. As Europe and the United States became stronger, the Islamic empires grew weaker. The Ottoman Empire, the last Islamic empire, lost power after World War I. European countries made some Muslim nations into colonies. During this time, the traditional arts of Islamic lands were nearly lost as European products flooded Asian and African markets.

Even with these hardships, however, Muslim artists worked to preserve their cultural traditions.

As Islamic countries began once again to gain their independence, they looked to their past to form a national identity. Today, Islamic artistic traditions are very much alive and help shape the culture of Muslims around the world.

The Aga Khan Award for Architecture was created in 1977 to honor architects whose work serves the needs of Muslim societies. Award winners often combine modern ideas

The Petronas Towers (connected buildings) at night

with Islamic traditions. Hassan Fathy of Egypt received the first Chairman's Award in 1980 for his energy-efficient designs that made use of mud bricks to provide housing for the poor.

An American architecture firm, Cesar Pelli and Associates, received the award in 2004 for the world's tallest buildings from 1996 to 2003, the Petronas Towers in Kuala Lumpur, Malaysia. The skyscrapers combine modern technology with a design grounded in Islamic tradition. The floor plan is based on two overlapping square shapes that form an eight-pointed star—an ancient Islamic pattern.

Truck drivers in Pakistan adorn their vehicles with colorful decorations based on traditional Islamic designs.

39

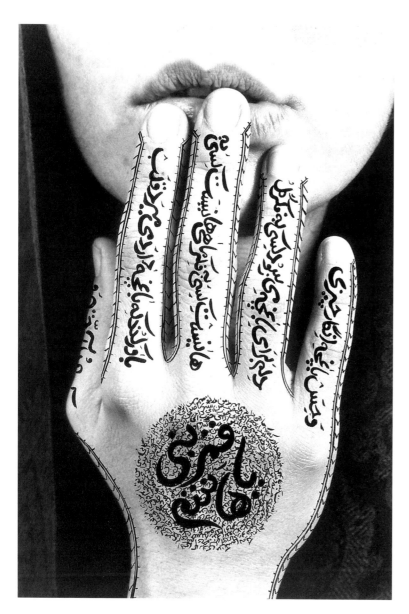

In recent years, Muslim women artists and writers have become well known for their work. Hanan al-Shaykh is a Lebanese writer whose novels, such as *The Story of Zahra*, focus on the experiences of Arab women. The Iranian-American artist Shirin Neshat uses photography and video to create powerful images that test the roles of women in Muslim society. Her work also draws attention to the ways Muslims are typecast in the West. Mona Hatoum is a Palestinian artist living in London. Her multimedia work often deals with having to live outside of her homeland because of war and troubles within the government.

Untitled (Women of Allah), 1996, by Shirin Neshat. Neshat combines photography and calligraphy to create images that often question Western views on Muslim women.

Some Muslim artists use traditional Islamic art forms like miniature painting and calligraphy to express modern ideas. Pakistani artist Shahzia Sikander uses politics, immigration, and the roles of men and women as subjects in her miniature paintings. Syrian artist Khaled al-Saai uses calligraphy to create his modern calligrams of landscapes and figures.

Pleasure Pillars, 2001, by Shahzia Sikander. Shahzia Sikander often uses handmade paper stained with tea and watercolors to create her miniature paintings.

American calligrapher Mohamed Zakariya created the first postage stamp to celebrate a Muslim holiday for the United States postal service. Zakariya used a reed pen and black ink for the calligraphy. His artwork was then colored in blue and gold on the computer.

Muslim singers and musicians have taken the world stage with music that often combines Middle Eastern, South Asian, and African sounds with elements from Western music. Baaba Maal started his career in Senegal when he served as the *muezzin* to call worshippers to prayer each day in his village. After studying in Paris, he began blending reggae and pop with Senegalese music in albums such as *Wango*, released in 1998.

Cheb Khaled is considered a pioneer of Rai music, which mixes Western and North African sounds. Khaled continues to develop his style of music by mixing jazz and hip-hop with Arabic lyrics. While Rai traces its roots to Algeria and Morocco, it came into being in France, which has many North African settlers.

Junoon was the first rock band to perform at the United Nations in New York City. The Pakistani group formed in 1990 and gained much attention when they were banned in Pakistan for criticizing the government in the late 1990s. They also angered some Muslims, who felt rock music did not fit in with the teachings of Islam. The band members

Baaba Maal performing in Mexico City in 2001

Starting from the left, Junoon band members Brian O'Connel, Salman Ahmed, and Ali Azmat pose in front of a public bus in Pakistan.

Ali Azmat, Salman Ahmed, and Brian O'Connel defend their music as being based on Sufi traditions and see no conflict between Islam and rock.

It has been nearly 1,400 years since the prophet Muhammad shared his vision of a new faith. Since then, the arts and sciences of Islam have deeply influenced the cultures of many nations. A lot of people in the West are unfamiliar with Islamic culture and the countless contributions it has made to the world. It is hoped this book will help change that.

Lebanese-American director Jehane Noujaim gained worldwide praise for her documentary *Control Room*. The film follows the crew members of Aljazeera, the Arab news network, as they cover the United States attack on Iraq in 2003. Noujaim compares the media coverage of the war from the different viewpoints of Americans and Arabs. In 2002, she and co-director Chris Hegedus won the award for Outstanding Directorial Achievement in Documentary for *Startup.Com* from the Directors Guild of America.

ca. 570 Muhammad is born

610 Muhammad starts the Islamic faith

622 Muhammad leaves Mecca for Yathrib, later Medina

630 Muhammad and followers conquer Mecca

632 Muhammad dies; Abu Bakr elected first caliph

661–750 Umayyad dynasty

661 Islamic capital is moved to Damascus

680 Muhammad's grandson Husayn and his family killed in the battle of Karbala

691 Dome of the Rock in Jerusalem completed

711 North African Muslims invade Spain

715 Great Mosque of Damascus completed

750–1258 Abbasid dynasty

756 Abd al-Rahman I, last Umayyad prince, reaches Spain and declares himself ruler

762 Baghdad becomes new Islamic capital

ca. 780 al-Khawarizmi born (d. ca. 850)

785 Great Mosque of Córdoba begun

800s Traders bring paper west from China; Islamic scholars translate works of Aristotle, Plato, and other ancient Greek thinkers; al-Khawarizmi (d. 850) lays down foundation for modern algebra

836 Samarra becomes Abbasid capital

mid-800s The One Thousand and One Nights first written down

909–1171 Fatimid dynasty

ca. 940 Abu'l Qasim Mansur (Firdausi) born (d. 1020)

970 Mosque of Al-Azhar built

980 Ibn Sena born (d. 1037)

1022 Ibn al-Bawwab dies

1038–1194 Seljuk dynasty

ca. 1141 Nazimi born (d. ca. 1217)

1048 Omar Khayyam born (d. 1122)

1055 Seljuks take over Baghdad

ca. 1095 Christian Crusades begin (end 1270)

ca. 1170 Mina'i pottery invented in Iran

1171–1250 Ayyubid dynasty

1184 Shaykh Muslihuddin Sa'di born (d. 1291)

1200s Koy Konboro builds Great Mosque of Djenne, Mali

1206 al-Jazari completes Al-Jami Bain Al-Ilm Wal-Amal Al-Nafi Fi Sinat'at Al-Hiyal

1206 Genghis Khan becomes leader of Mongols

1207 Jelaluddin Rumi born (d. 1273)

1230–1492 Nasrid dynasty

1238 Córdoba returns to Christian rule

1247 Rashid al-Din born (d. 1317)

mid-1200s Work begins on the Alhambra in Granada, Spain

1250–1517 Mamluk dynasty

1256–1336 Ilkhanid dynasty

1258 Mongols conquer Baghdad, ending Abbasid dynasty

1281–1924 Ottoman dynasty founded

late 1200s Muslim merchants from India bring Islam to Indonesia

1300s Qawaali, a Sufi form of music, begins in India

1304 Ibn Battuta born (d. 1369)

1370–1501 Timurid dynasty

ca. 1440 Kamal-uddin Bihzad born (d. ca. 1536)

1453 Ottomans conquer Constantinople

1489 Mimar Sinan born (d. 1588)

1492 Christian forces drive the Muslims out of Spain

early 1500s Zahiruddin Muhammad Babur conquers India

1500s Iznik in Anatolia becomes famous for its pottery

1501–1732 Safavid dynasty

1520 Suleyman becomes leader of Ottomans

1526–1857 Mughal dynasty is founded in India

ca. 1550 Mansur born (d. ca. 1630)

1590s Safavid capital moves to Isfahan

1617 Mu'in Musavvir born (d. 1708); Mosque of Sultan Ahmet I (the Blue Mosque) in Constantinople completed

1647 Taj Mahal in Agra, India, completed

1779–1924 Qajar dynasty

1900 Hassan Fathy born (d. 1989)

1942 Mohamed Zakariya born

1945 Hanan al-Shaykh born

1948 Nusrat Fateh Ali Khan is born (d. 1997)

1954 Baaba Maal born

1957 Shirin Neshat, Mona Hatoum born

1960 Cheb Khaled born

1969 Shahzia Sikander born

1970 Khaled al-Saai born

1975 Jehane Noujaim born

1977 Aga Khan Award for Architecture created

1990 Brian O'Connel, Salman Ahmed, and Ali Azmat form the rock band Junoon

1996 Petronas Towers in Kuala Lumpur, Malaysia, named highest building in the world (surpassed in 2003 by Taipei 101 in Taiwan)

arabesque a pattern of interlaced lines that trace the outlines of flowers, leaves, fruits, and other natural shapes

artisan a craftsperson

caliph a leader of Islam, regarded as a successor of Muhammad

calligram a picture of an animal, object, or other figure that is made by using calligraphy

calligraphy the art of decorative handwriting

caravansary a large inn built along trade routes in central and western Asia

dynasty a series of rulers who belong to the same family

geometric patterns and designs based on circles, squares, stars, and other shapes

hadith the collected sayings of Muhammad on the meaning of the Qur'an

hajj the trip to Mecca required of all Muslims

madrassa a Muslim religious school

Mamluks slave soldiers who could serve in important government offices and were often paid; also a Muslim dynasty from 1256 to 1336

medallion a design used in carpet making that looks like a large medal, often placed in the center

mihrab an alcove in the wall of a mosque that shows the direction of Mecca

minaret a tower attached to a mosque from which a muezzin calls people to prayer

mosaic a picture made up of small pieces of stone, glass, or tile cemented in place

mosque a place of worship for Muslims

muezzin the crier who calls Muslims to prayer five times a day

niello black enamel used to fill a carved design

prophet a person who has visions that impart a message from God; also a religious leader who shares this vision

qibla the direction of the Ka'aba, which Muslims face when praying

Qur'an the sacred text of Islam that contain the revelations of God to Muhammad; also known as the Koran

rock crystal a colorless, transparent, semiprecious gemstone

scholar a learned person

shrine a place where someone can go to pray or pay tribute to a holy person

FURTHER READING

Cathryn Clinton, *Stone in My Hand*, Candlewick Press, 2002

Lucille Davis, *The Ottoman Empire* (Life During the Great Civilizations), Blackbirch Press, 2003

Aisha Karen Khan, *What You Will See Inside a Mosque*, Skylight Paths Publishing, 2003

Rukhsana Khan, *Muslim Child: Understanding Islam through Stories and Poems*, Albert Whitman, 2002

Demi, *Muhammad*, Simon & Schuster, 2003

David Macaulay, *Mosque*, Houghton Mifflin, 2003

Elsa Marston, *Muhammad of Mecca: Prophet of Islam*, Scholastic, 2002

Neil Morris, *The Atlas of Islam: People, Daily Life and Traditions*, Barron's Educational Series, 2003

Sue Penney, *Islam*, Heinemann Library, 2000

Philip Wilkinson, *Islam* (Eyewitness Books Series), DK Publishing, 2005

Web Sites

PBS
Empire of Faith: Islam
http://www.pbs.org/empires/islam

The Detroit Institute of Arts
Ancient Art: Islamic Art
http://www.dia.org/collections/ancient/islamicart/islamicart.html

BBC
Introduction to Islamic Art
http://www.bbc.co.uk/religion/religions/islam/features/art/index.shtml

A

Abbasid Caliphs, Tomb of the, 16
Abbasid caliphs, 16, 20
Abbasid dynasty, 10, 12–13, 17, 18
Abbasi, Reza, 32
Abbas, Kusam ibn, 27
Abbas, Shah, 32
Abraham, 6
Adam, 6
Afghanistan, 27
Africa, 5, 10, 12, 14–19, 21, 23
Afsharid dynasty, 33
Aga Khan Award for Architecture, 38–39
Agha, Sedefkâr Mehmet, 30
Agra, India, 36
agriculture, 11
Ahmed, Salman, 43
Ahmed, Shiblizade, 31
Ahmet I, 30
Akbar, 34, 36
al-Andalus (Islamic Spain), 11
al-Bawwab, Ibn, 7
Algeria, 14
Alhambra, 10–11
al-Azhar University, 14
al-Din, Rashid, 26
al-Din, Salah (Saladin), 16
Algeria, 42
Ali (Muhammad's son-in-law), 9
Aljazeera, 43
al-Khawarizmi, 12
al-Malik, Abd, 8
al-Mutadibih, 12
al-Mutawakkil, 13
al-Qahira (Cairo), 14, 16, 18, 19
al-Jazari, 20
al-Rahman I, Abd, 10
al-Saai, Khaled, 41
al-Shaykh, Hanan, 40
al Walid, 9
al-Malik, Abd, 8
Anatolia (Turkey), 20, 23, 26, 30, 31
Arabia, 4, 5, 11, 13, 19, 30
Arabs, 28
arabesques, 13, 19, 29
architecture, 5, 6, 7–8, 10–11, 12, 13, 14, 17, 27, 29, 30, 31, 36–37, 38–39
Asia, 5, 12, 20–27
Aristotle, 12
astronomy, 12, 22

Azmat, Ali, 43
Ayyubid dynasty, 16–17, 19

B

Babur, Zahiruddin Muhammad, 34
Baghdad, 12, 13, 16, 20, 24
Bakr, Abu, 9
Battuta, Ibn, 19
Beyezid II, 29
Bey, Sinan, 31
Bible, 16
Bihzad, Kamal-uddin, 32
Black Stone, 6
Blue Mosque, 30
book-making, 33
books, 4, 5, 33

C

Cairo (al-Qahira), 14, 16, 18, 19
calligraphy, 4, 5, 7, 18, 20, 33, 40, 41
Cappadocia, 21
caravansaries, 21
carpets, 19, 25, 28–29
carving, 15, 16, 18
Cesar Pelli and Associates, 39
China, 5, 12, 13, 19, 20, 24, 25
city planning, 12
clothing, 29
Córdoba, 10
court artists, 34–35
Crusades, 15, 16, 23

D

Damascus, 8, 9, 16, 21
dervishes, 23
Djenné, 17
Dome of the Rock, 8

E

education, 12
Egypt, 14, 15, 16, 18, 30
Europe, 12, 15, 20, 21, 22, 23, 24, 30, 35, 38

F

Fathy, Hassan, 39
Fatimid dynasty, 14–15, 16
Ferdinand, King, 11
figurative painting, 4, 7, 9, 26
film, documentary, 41
Firdausi (Abu'l Qasim Mansur), 22, 24
Five Pillars of Islam, 6
foods, 11

France, 42

G

Gabriel (Jibra'il), 4, 7, 8
gardens, 36–37
geometric designs, 13
Ghaznavid dynasty, 20
Ghazan, 24
glassware, 16, 18, 19
Granada, 10
Great Mosque of Córdoba, 10
Great Mosque of Damascus, 9
Great Mosque of Djenne, 17

H

Hadith, 7
Hagia Sofia, 30
Hajj, 6
Hatoum, Mona, 40
Herat, 27, 32
Hülegü, 13, 24
Hungary, 24
Hussein (Muhammad's grandson), 9

I

Ilkhanid dynasty, 24–26
India, 5, 12, 13, 14, 19, 27, 28, 32, 34–37
Indonesia, 37
inventions, 20
Iran, 5, 13, 20, 21, 22, 24, 27, 28, 32, 33, 34, 36
Iraq, 12, 15, 20, 21, 27
irrigation systems, 11
Isabella, Queen, 11
Islam, birth of, 4
Istanbul, 31
Italy, 19
Iznik, 31

J

Jahan, Shah, 36
Jehangir, 35, 36
Jerusalem, 8, 15, 16
jewelry, 15, 25, 31
Jibra'il (Gabriel), 4, 7, 8
Junoon, 43

K

Ka'aba, 6, 8
Karbala, battle of, 9
Khaled, Cheb, 42
Khan, Genghis, 13, 24, 26
Khan, Kublai, 24
Khan, Nusrat Fateh Ali, 35

Khanum, Bibi, 27
Khatun, Rabia, 16
Khayyam, Omar, 22
Konboro, Koy, 17
Koran (Qur'an), 7, 9, 18
Kuala Lumpur, 39

L

literature, 5, 12, 13, 18, 19, 22–23, 26, 32, 40
London, 28, 40

M

Maal, Baba, 42
madrassa, 16, 27, 31
Mahal, Mumtaz, 36
Malaysia, 39
Mali, 17
Mamluk dynasty, 17, 18–19, 30
Mansur, 35
Mansur, Abu'l Qasim (Firdausi), 22, 24
mathematics, 12, 22
Mecca, 4, 5, 6, 8, 10, 19
medicine, 22
Medina, 5, 6, 8
Mediterranean Sea, 14, 18
Mehmet II, 30, 31
metalwork, 5, 16, 18, 20
Mevlevi dervishes, 23
Mexico City, 42
Middle Ages, 12
mihrab, 8, 10
minarets, 8–9, 17
Mongolia, 24
Mongols, 13, 16, 18, 24–27, 28, 30
Morocco, 19
mosaics, 9
Mosque of Sultan Hasan, 19
mosques, 9, 10, 12, 14, 17, 19, 27, 30, 31
Mosul, 21
muezzin, 9, 42
Mughal dynasty, 34–37
Muhammad, 4, 5, 6, 7, 8, 9, 26, 27, 43
Muharram, 9
Mu'in, 32
music, 5, 11, 23, 34, 35, 42–43

N

Nasrid dynasty, 10
Nazimi, 32
Neshat, Shirin, 40
New York City, 43

nomads, 25, 28
Noujaim, Jehane, 41

O

O'Connel, Brian, 43
Ottomans, 4, 29, 30–31, 38

P

painting, 29, 32
paintings, miniature, 4, 12, 23, 24, 26, 29, 31, 32, 33, 34, 35, 40–41
Pakistan, 28, 43
palaces, 12, 14, 25, 27, 30
paper, introduction of, 12
Peacock Throne, 36, 37
Petronas Towers, 39
photography, 40
Plato, 12
pottery, 5, 15, 16, 18, 21, 25, 31, 38

Q

Qajar dynasty, 33
Qibla, 6
Qur'an (Koran), 7, 9, 18, 31, 37

R

Ramadan, 6
realism, European, 33
Rembrandt, 35
rock crystal, 15
Rumi, Jelaluddin, 23

S

Sa'di, Shaykh Muslihuddin, 23
Safavid dynasty, 30, 32–33
Safavi, Isma'il, 32
Saladin (Salah al-Din), 16, 17
Samarkand, 27
Samarra, 13
Saudi Arabia, 4
science, 5, 11, 12, 20, 22
Selim I, 30
Seljuk dynasty, 20–21, 28, 30
Sena, Ibn, 22
Senegal, 42
shadow puppets, 37
Shah, Fath Ali, 33
Shah-i Zinda, 27
Shajahanabad, 36
Shi'i, 9, 16, 32
Sicily, 14
Sikander, Shahzia, 40
Silk Road, 20
Sinan, Mimar, 30, 31

slave soldiers, 17
Southeast Asia, 5
Spain, 5, 10–11
Strait of Gibraltar, 10
Sufism, 23, 35
Sufi traditions, 43
Suleymaniye Mosque, 31
Suleyman the Magnificent, 30
Sunni, 9, 16, 32
Syria, 8, 11, 15, 16, 18, 26, 30

T

Tabriz, 24, 32
Taj Mahal, 36–37
Takht-i Sulaiman palace, 25
Tamerlane (Timur), 26–27
Tangier, 19
tents, 25
textiles, 5, 19, 21, 25, 28–29
Tigris River, 12
tiles, 25, 30
Timur (Tamerlane), 26–27, 34
Timurid dynasty, 26–27, 32
Topkapi palace, 30, 31
trade, 14, 15, 20, 35
Tunisia, 14
Turkey, 4, 17, 20, 21, 29, 32

U

Umayyad dynasty, 8–9, 10–11
United Nations, 43
United States, 38, 41
Uzbekistan, 27

V

Venice, 19
Victoria & Albert Museum, 28
vision, 4

W

weaving, 28–29
whirling dervishes, 23
World War I, 38

Y

Yamuna River, 36
Yathrib, 4
Yemen, 16

Z

Zakariya, Mohamed, 41
Zand dynasty, 33
zodiac signs, 21
Zuljana, 9

ACKNOWLEDGMENTS

The editors wish to thank the following organizations and individuals for permission to reprint the literary quotes and to reproduce the images in this book. Every effort has been made to obtain permission from the owners of all materials. Any errors that may have been made are unintentional and will be corrected in future printings if notice is given to the publisher.

Cover (left): *Deep bowl*/Iran or Afghanistan, 10th century/Glazed earthenware/H: 11.2 Diam: 39.3 cm/Freer Gallery of Art, Smithsonian Institution, Washington, D.C.: Purchase, F1957.24; **(right):** *Bowl*/Iran, late 12th–early 13th century/Stonepaste body painted over glaze with enamel (mina'i)/H: 8.8 W: 23.0 D: 23.0 cm/ Freer Gallery of Art, Smithsonian Institution, Washington, D.C.: Purchase, F1938.12

Title page, p. 8: The Dome of the Rock/Ablestock

Contents: Photograph © Atif Toor

p. 4: The Archangel Gabriel inspires Muhammad/Turkish painting, 16th century/The Art Archive/Turkish and Islamic Art Museum, Istanbul/HarperCollins Publishers

p. 5: Metalwork calligraphy ornament/Photograph © Atif Toor

p. 6: Muslims circle the Ka'aba/Khaled el Fiqi/EPA Photos/Newscom

p. 7: Page of Qur'an/School of Yakurt el Musta'simi/Ayyubid dynasty/The Art Archive/Museum of Islamic Art, Cairo/Dagli Orti

p. 9 (top): Interior wall mosaic, Great Mosque of Damascus, Syria/Umayyad dynasty/The Art Archive/Dagli Orti; **(bottom):** Contemporary wall painting of Zuljana, Muhammad's horse/Photograph © Atif Toor

p. 10: Detail of *mihrab*, Great Mosque of Córdoba, Spain/The Art Archive/Dagli Orti

p. 11 (top): Court of the Lions, Alhambra, Granada, Spain/The Art Archive/Dagli Orti; **(bottom):** Oranges and lemons on Moroccan dish/Photograph © Atif Toor

p. 12: Anatomy of the eye, from 1214 manuscript by al-Mutadibih/The Art Archive/Egyptian Museum, Cairo/Dagli Orti

p. 13 (right): Great Mosque of al-Mutawakkil, Samarra, Iraq/Abbasid dynasty/The Art Archive/Dagli Orti; **(bottom):** Sinbad and the Old Man of the Sea from 1399 manuscript, probably Baghdad/The Art Archive/The Bodleian Library, Oxford (Bodley Or 133, folio 43r)

p. 14: Central court of al-Azhar Mosque, Cairo, Egypt/Fatimid dynasty/The Art Archive/Dagli Orti

p. 15 (top): Rock crystal ewer/10th century/Fatimid dynasty/The Art Archive/Palazzo Pitti, Florence/Dagli Orti; **(bottom):** Fatimid troops leaving fortress at Ascalon to attack Crusaders/Paper fragment from Fustat, Egypt/12th century/The Art Archive/British Museum

p. 16: Canteen/Syria or northern Iraq, mid-13th century/Brass, silver inlay/H: 45.2 W: 36.7 D: 21.5 cm/ Freer Gallery of Art, Smithsonian Institution, Washington, D.C.: Purchase, F1941.10

p. 17 (right): *Portrait of Saladin* (1138–93) (color litho)/Arabic School/British Library, London, UK/Bridgeman Art Library; **(bottom):** Great Mosque of Djenné/Andrew Gilham/www.andygilham.com

p. 18: Fairuz at the pond with the king of elephants, from 1354 manuscript *Kalila wa Dimna*/Mamluk dynasty/possibly Syrian/The Art Archive/The Bodleian Library, Oxford (Pococke 400, folio 99r)

p. 19: Enameled glass lamp/16th century/Sultan Hasan Mosque, Cairo, Egypt/The Art Archive/Museum of Islamic Art, Cairo/Dagli Orti

p. 20: Fountain with mechanism for raising water, from 1206 Seljuk manuscript *The Book of Knowledge of Ingenious Mechanical Devices* by al-Jazari, inventor/The Art Archive/Topkapi Museum, Istanbul/Dagli Orti

p. 21 (top): Sultan Han Caravansary, Cappadocia, Turkey/The Art Archive/Dagli Orti; **(bottom):** Bowl, late 12th–early 13th century; Seljuq, Central or northern Iran, *Mina'i* ware, composite body, opaque white glaze with gilding, overglaze painting; H. 3 3/4 in. (9.5 cm), Diam. 7 3/8 in. (18.7 cm)/The Metropolitan Museum of Art, Purchase, Rogers Fund, and Gift of The Schiff Foundation, 1957 (57.36.4) Photograph © 1994 The Metropolitan Museum of Art

p. 22: "In your light I learn how to love" (excerpt) by Jelalludin Rumi, translation © Coleman Barks/Courtesy of Coleman Barks; 14th-century copy of *Canon of Medicine* by Ibn Sena (Avicenna)/Damascus, Syria/The Art Archive/National Museum, Damascus, Syria/Dagli Orti

p. 23 (top): Dervishes dancing during preparation of a meal, from *Bustan or Gulistan* by Sa'di, ca. 1580–90/The Art Archive/The Bodleian Library, Oxford (Laud. OR.241, folio 1b-2a); **(bottom):** Ud player, painted ceramic plate/11th century/Fustat, Egypt/The Art Archive/Museum of Islamic Art, Cairo/Dagli Orti

p. 24: Genghis Khan (1167–1227) fighting Chinese in mountains, from *Shahnama* by Firdausi/1397/Timurid dynasty/The Art Archive/British Library

p. 25 (top): Frieze tile with phoenix, ca. 1270s, Iran (probably Takht-i Sulayman), Fritware, overglaze luster-painted; 14 3/4 x 14 1/4 in. (37.5 x 36.2 cm)/The Metropolitan Museum of Art, Rogers Fund, 1912 (12.49.4). Photograph © 1993 The Metropolitan Museum of Art; **(bottom):** Gold leaf bracelet with turquoise/14th century/Mongol Empire/from Nejzac treasure/The Art Archive/Hermitage Museum, Saint Petersburg/Dagli Orti

p. 26: Cavalry attack of Persian army, which actually shows arms and armor of Mongol army, from *Collected Histories* by Rashid al-Din/The Art Archive/Edinburgh University Library

p. 27: Shah-i Zinda, Samarkand, Uzbekistan/The Library of Congress

p. 28: Ardabil carpet. Safavid. 1539–40. Woolen pile on silk warp and weft. 10.52 x 5.33 m (CT 1432)/Victoria and Albert Museum, London/Art Resource, NY

p. 29: Robe belonging to Ottoman ruler Bayezid II (1447/8–1512)/The Art Archive/Topkapi Museum, Istanbul/Dagli Orti

p. 30: The Mosque of Sultan Ahmet I (Blue Mosque), Istanbul, Turkey/The Art Archive/Dagli Orti

p. 31 (top): *Sultan Mehmet II* (1432–81) shown holding a rose, ca. 1475, attributed to Sinan Bey/The Art Archive/Topkapi Museum, Istanbul/Dagli Orti; **(bottom):** Book binding, gold encrusted with precious stones/16th century/The Art Archive/Topkapi Museum, Istanbul/Dagli Orti

p. 32: Harun al-Rashid at the barber, from *Khamsa* by Nazimi, painted by Kamal-uddin Bihzad/The Art Archive/British Library

p. 33 (right): *Fath' Ali Shah* (1771–1834), King of Persia, Mirza Baba (fl. 1780–1830), Private Collection/Bridgeman Art Library; **(bottom):** 1650 Persian manuscript/The Art Archive/Museum of Islamic Art, Cairo/Dagli Orti

p. 34: Court scene before Mughal Emperor Akbar, with Chaghatai Turk dancers/Gouache miniature, ca. 1565/The Art Archive/The Bodleian Library, Oxford (Douce OR.b1, folio 12V)

p. 35 (top): *Blue-throated Barber*, Ustad Mansur/The Art Archive/Victoria and Albert Museum, London/Eileen Tweedy; **(bottom):** Nusrat Fateh Ali Khan/HO/Reuters Photo Archive/Newscom

p. 36: *Mughal Emperor Shah Jahan* (1592–1666) on Peacock Throne/Late 18th century/The Art Archive/Victoria and Albert Museum, London/Sally Chappell

p. 37 (top): The Taj Mahal, Agra, India/The Art Archive/Dagli Orti; **(bottom):** Shadow puppets, Indonesia/Punchstock

p. 38: Artist painting ceramic vase/Photograph © Atif Toor

p. 39 (top): The Petronas Towers, Kuala Lumpur, Malaysia/Karam Adle/EPA Photos/Newscom; **(bottom):** Painted Pakistani truck/Photograph © Atif Toor

p. 40: Shirin Neshat/*Untitled* (Women of Allah)/1996/Black & white photograph with ink/Photo by Larry Barns/9 3/8 x 6 1/2 inches (23.8 x 16.5 cm)/Copyright Shirin Neshat 1996/Courtesy Gladstone Gallery, New York

p. 41 (top): Shahzia Sikander/*Pleasure Pillars*/2001/Color, tea, ink on hand-prepared wasli paper/12 x 10 inches/Courtesy Brent Sikkema NYC; **(bottom):** Eid postage stamp/United States Postal Service

p. 42: Baaba Maal/José Luis Ramirez Negrete/Agencia Reforma/Newscom

p. 43 (top): Junoon band members/www.junoon.com; **(bottom):** Jehane Noujaim at 54th Annual DGA Awards/Vince Bucci/Getty/Newscom

Backgrounds, pp. 4, 8–9, 12 (book), 34, 36, 42: Ablestock

Backgrounds, pp. 14, 29 (fabric), and all sidebar backgrounds: Photographs © Atif Toor